OK, YOU'VE F'D UP!
NOW WHAT?

OK, YOU'VE F'D UP!
NOW WHAT?

Crossroad Moments:
A PATHWAY TO SUCCESS

TA-MUK SCRUGGS

Ok, You've F'd Up! Now What?

Copyright © 2018 Ta-Muk Scruggs, all rights reserved. No part of this book may be reproduced or transmitted in any form or by any means, electronic or mechanical, including photocopying, recording or by any information storage and retrieval system without written permission from the author.

PUB ISBN #978-0578-42410-1
EPUB ISBN #978-0578-42411-8

Printed in the United States of America

This book is about taking the steps needed to STILL have a good life, AFTER making mistakes, by being real with yourself and making decisions that take you down a different and better path for your life.

\#

There are moments when life will pose a question to you. How you answer, will determine which direction your life will go and ultimately how you will turn out. I call these moments, "CROSSROADS" moments, because you get to a point on your life path, where you can go left or right, but, you can never go back. You become a new person, sometimes better, sometimes worse, depending on your decision.

These "CROSSROADS" moments have a tendency to take you in a circle. A circle simply because the Holy Universe/God has a lesson for you to learn. Far too often, we repeat this circle of a path. Even more often, we get trapped on this path, and it's normally the path that turns us towards being a worse individual with each trip down this path versus a better, higher version of ourselves. We often walk this path so long that we dig ourselves a path so deep, that we can't get out of the hole we've dug for ourselves.

Sometimes though we take the path that takes us directly to our next stage of EVOLUTION and to our higher, ENLIGHTENED self. Here lies the question; how does one know which path to take and since either path teaches us a lesson, how can one be right versus wrong?

The paths aren't right or wrong! One may be shorter than the other in helping you get to understanding the lesson, but, neither is right or wrong. The paths teach you a lesson about your life, character, morality, and LOVE. One just so happens to have a repeat button for those of us who are, let's just say "COMPRHENSIONALLY CHALLENGED"!

Being stubborn, egotistical, prideful, and closed-minded, causes one to take the path that we know is more than likely to be the easiest path for us. Yet and still, like so many, before us, that chose the path with the "repeat" button, we all choose it like we are the one who can "beat the system". The problem is, NO-BODY-EVER-BEATS-THE-SYSTEM!

With that being said, if you follow these steps, YOU WILL BECOME SUCCESSFUL in whatever area you choose for your life. So grab you a good beverage and a great snack. Find you someplace peaceful. Grab a highlighter, pen and paper to take notes, and change your own F'N LIFE for the better! You deserve it! You have suffered far too long. You have the strength to do this! Do yourself and your family the biggest favor you could ever do for them—ELEVATE THEM and ELEVATE YOURSELF!

I do not know who you are, but should you want to share your story from where you are when you began this book, to where you hope to go or where it has helped you get to, then you can email me your story and a picture or pictures of your success to OKIFUKDUP@gmail.com and maybe I'll share your story when I speak to others who need to hear your story of living beyond your mistakes. Until then, enjoy and let nothing stop you!

#ANYTHINGISPOSSIBLE

Contents

Work Out (Physically) 1

Work Out (Mentally) 3

It Just Be Callin' Me! (Vices) 7

A Fool Knows Everything! The Wiseman Knows
He Knows Nothing! (Study, Study, Study) 11

A 20 Year Plan For A 100 Year Reign (Patience) 13

Are You Your Biggest Cheerleader Or
Your Own Biggest Hater (Be Positive) 19

Do As I Say. . . . (Be And Stay Positive) 23

Always Be Polite! Even To The Assholes (Stay Humble) 27

Can You Even Find A Hat For That Head (Ego) 31

Your Net-Work Is Your Net-Worth! (Network) 35

Excuse Me Brutha But Errrruh,
You Got Some Spare Change (Giving) 37

Work Out (Physically)

Studies have shown that exercising for at least an hour a day, will extend your life by a minimum of ten years. How is that relative you may ask? Well, think about it like this; while your friends are out here smoking cigarettes, smoking weed, drinking hard liquor, and staying up partying all night, they are cutting their ability to: create ten years of memories, experience vacations to exotic locations, grow their generational wealth, expand their land ownership, and increase their power to create positive changes for their families, friends, and community.

That should be all of our goal! Our goal, every day, should be, to be here long enough to create the best opportunities for our LOVED ones, and also be here to PHYSICALLY enjoy these opportunities.

It's amazing how even at the minimum of walking briskly, for sixty minutes a day, we are ADDING TIME to our lives. It is hard to understand how one does not decide to "get up and move" like it is said in the ads by former first lady Michelle Obama, or by countless sports stars.

I mean really, have you not seen their bodies?! Look at Serena Williams, Misty Copeland, and LeBron James! All of them are wonderfully carved, physically fit, and flexible human beings! Yes, they have professional trainers and money to afford trainers and time to focus on working out hours at a time.

Here's the thing though, YOU ARE NOT TRYING TO BE A SPORTS STAR! So you don't have to work out as much as they do, or, spend the amount of time and money that they spend working out, but you can still look and be fit just like them. You only need to invest your time, energy, and a very small amount of money in order to get fit and stay in shape.

It only takes a dollar to buy a gallon of water. Spend two dollars, and now, not only do you have an eight pound weight to carry around, or do curls with, but, you also have a second one to keep you from passing out from being dehydrated while carrying around a gallon of water all day working out! See, that's what you call a "WIN-WIN"! You've worked out and you've drank a gallon of water, all in one day! This all contributes to the longevity of your life and guess what, it only cost you TWO DOLLARS to do it! So now what? What's your excuse now, "Mr. / Mrs. Tight Pockets"?

Work Out (Mentally)

ONE OF THE other "health" benefits of working out, is, how it affects your brain. The more you work out, the better your blood circulates. The better blood circulation you have, the more oxygen you get to those precious brain cells.

Oxygen to the brain causes faster, better, clearer decisions to be made. This allows you to focus better on accomplishing your goals, whether they be short-term (immediate) goals or long-term (future) goals.

Some of the things that should be done, along with exercising your body is exercising your mind. Now, I know this has become extremely hard now with the creation of the internet and the full time access to both reality shows (for women), porn (for men), and video games (for children)—and yes, all of these things will teach you things and create thoughts, but come on, who are we kidding here! Who really cares about what guy Kim K and/or her dad is dating?! Who really cares about the next version of Call of Duty? Seriously, why is it that anyone would like to see lesbian midgets performing BDSM? Yes, I know that there are many of viewers for all of those different distractions, but, how will this help enhance your life? How will any of these things help you to become successful? How will any of these things help to make your loved one's future brighter? The sad reality is, for most of us, THEY DON'T! They are simply a distraction from your problems, life, and success, or lack thereof.

So how do you break out or away from the mind numbing dribble of the TV? The first and easiest way is to pick up and read a book! Not just any book! Find and read something that will allow your mind to think and grow beyond its current capacity. Better still, find books that will teach you about the technical aspects of what you TRULY love to do. Doing so will bring you that much more joy, happiness, and LOVE! These are the things that start and continuously cause those brain cells to fire at their max and best levels!

Have you ever seen an athlete get that "look" in their eyes? You know that "look" of "OH YEAH! I'M TUNED IN!", "NOTHING CAN STOP ME NOW!", "I'M UNSTOPPABLE!", "I'M A BEAST!".

Michael Jordan had it when he threw in 63 points to win a championship. Michael Phelps had it when he won six gold medals in the Olympics. Serena Williams had it on her face and in her screams as she won her record setting sixth grand slam title!

These are world class athletes! In top physical form! They all are known for their focus during moments when good isn't good enough, but where "GREATNESS" is expected and demanded in order for there to be success at the highest level.

We all have this ability. We can do it in our daily lives.

People who read books on Yoga and practice Tai-Chi, often try to achieve a higher state of mind. They understand the mental and physical benefits of "working out" your mind.

Other examples of exercising mentally are meditation, art, music, and dance. These things allow your mind to float beyond the common surroundings, whether it be the noise and chaos at home, at school, at work, or in your hood.

Buddah, Picasso, Prince, Misty Copeland all were known for being able to help others transport themselves beyond their physical surroundings through their works.

It is said that the more one creates, the more one can imagine. So when you pick up a pencil and paper, an instrument, even a welder, you are potentially unlocking your minds deepest thoughts. Tapping into your subconscious allows you to look into the future. It helps you to "SEE" all the steps, plans, actions, RE-actions, to all the moves needed to reach your end goal.

A great example of this was showcased in the Sherlock Holmes' movies. His mind was so focused that he could see both his moves, as well as, his opponent's moves, allowing him to be victorious over them even before their fights.

There are moments in life where you'll be faced with situations that will require your deepest, most focused attention. These moments could be life altering! They could even be decisions that could save life or cost a life. So one should be prepared for these moments. This means that one most exercise the brain every day, just like one should exercise the body, for a minimum of an hour a day.

Be limitless!

It Just Be Callin' Me! (Vices)

Addiction and/or vices, the things that we do, knowingly and unknowingly, that keep us from being successful, are some of the biggest obstacles to overcome.

Some start out as something simple, like a wine cooler, a five dollar weed joint, or even just something meant to be fun and, like a simple game of twenty five cent "TUNK". Some start out at an early age smoking cigarettes or having sex or even stealing candy from the corner store.

All of these things can lead to bigger, more costly, life altering addictions. Some even lead to jail, or worse, death, which could be the worst outcome for us all!

Other types of addictions or vices in the next case is the vice of holding on to things that need to be let go of, but can't be bought at a store like cigarettes, weed, or alcohol. These addictions and vices are mental. They occur from situations like physical abuse, sexual abuse, and depression.

Have you ever seen someone do something bad or negative even though they know that doing it isn't good for them physically or mentally. For example, watching someone taking mental and physical abuse, all while saying they love their abuser. After a certain point, it no longer is the abuser's responsibility to stop the bad behavior, but, it is the abused responsibility to bring it to an end. Have you ever watched an obese person workout, and then head straight for the fast food place immediately after that workout?!

These people are addicted! Yet they wonder how come they are still in bad relationships or can't lose the weight they NEED to lose. It takes a strong support system and an even stronger desire to live happy and healthy. Doing the first two steps of physically and mentally working out drastically improve your chances of letting go of any vices that one has.

One of the hardest vices to break the grip on us is involving ourselves with loved ones' life problems. Now you may not be strung out on crack, or tweeking for a weed hit, but, what you may find yourself doing is always trying to fix and solve others problems. A lot of these situations can easily be resolved by the actual individual but you find yourself interjecting and giving unsolicited advice. Doing this, brings the same intense, but temporary, rush that drugs bring users. You end up chasing that rush. An idea here, a suggestion there, your two cents to a conversations that never involved you at all.

Learning to breathe, long, deep breathes, and meditating on what is most meaningful to you in your life helps making letting go easier. It may take some time to accomplish due to the level of love for and close connection to the vice, but, in the end, being able to break the stronghold grip on you will be well worth it. This will allow you to make tough, unbiased, decisions for the success of your life, and it won't be clouded by emotions or any mind altering drugs, or the blocking of positive thoughts that get destroyed by alcohol.

A free and clear mind allows our conscious and subconscious to expand exponentially. Removing vices like drugs, alcohol, sex, ego, and pride will help you imagine the big picture and keep you focused on the next steps to getting you to your successful plateau.

A Fool Knows Everything! The Wiseman Knows He Knows Nothing! (Study, Study, Study)

ONCE YOU STARTED and used to doing these other steps, take the time to read and study! And don't just read anything! Read things that will increase your understanding. Read about the things you are in love with and passionate about. All the great and successful people in every field have taken the time to read and study about the things they love and want to be, not just successful at, but GREAT at. It's true that it is better to have a bigger library than a bigger TV.

The more you read, study, and experience, the more questions you have will be answered. Ultimately though, this leads to further questions. What this does is makes you fluent in your particular field or life. It also allows you to be able to confidently converse with other experts who will want to make sure that you not only know about what they are talking about, but that you are worth their investment in you.

Studies show that those who continue their education beyond high school do better in life that those who only get a high school diploma or G.E.D. Studies also show that those who go out and apply what they've learned through schools like college or trade schools, do even better than just a standard education. There's a reason why employers don't hire people with just a diploma or degrees. These things may get you looked at, but, what companies are looking for to continue growing and making their business successful is those individuals who have not only studied a/any particular thing(s), but, are also out in the world applying and implementing these changes.

Every "expert" became an "expert" by taking their raw talent and coupling that with a mentor of "expert" level in their field. They then studied the "experts" techniques and took the best lessons for themselves and left the things alone that didn't work for them.

They say it takes approximately ten thousand hours of practice to become an expert at something. That's a one and four zeros! Now seeing how the average work day is eight hours, hey, well, you do the math! That's a lot of days, and they get longer the more you study and the longer you spend studying. And, like we discussed earlier, the more you study, the more questions get answered, but the more questions arise.

The thing is, as you answer more questions, your love for those questions will increase, and as such, your income will do the same. Increasing your income increases your ability to create opportunities and experiences for happiness, for yourself, your loved ones, and others who are dedicated to doing better in the world and FOR the world.

A 20 Year Plan For
A 100 Year Reign
(Patience)

A FEW YEARS AGO, I was in the process of trying to get my life on track. I was attending a program for fathers who wanted to improve their relationships with their families and communities. I was taking a tax prep class through one of the biggest tax companies out here. I was actively looking for work. I was doing it all by the way of the bus and the kindness of family and friends. Once I was finally able to save up and get a car, I moved my efforts along significantly. However, not having a driver's license still had me in the very bad position of do I drive and risk getting tickets, points, and even worse going to jail, or, do I throw caution to the wind and try to earn my own independence. So I did what a judge said seventy-five percent of people in Michigan did—DRIVE! EVERY DAY! EVERY WHERE! This eventually caught up with me, as I ended up getting stopped and arrested and had to go in front of an unforgiving and uncaring judge in the suburbs, where black men didn't fair well, with or without a lawyer, which I wasn't able to afford.

This particular judge felt that mu continued driving was a direct slap in the face to the law and herself, personally! She didn't care about any of the positive things I had going on and/or was trying to do to fix my own life. She ended up sentencing me to ninety days in jail! I was PISSED! I was mad at her, at myself, at the entire justice system. She sent me to the county jail and from there I was moved to the "TRUSTEE" camp, a low level security facility where you could earn days off your sentence by doing work for the county. Me being so angry, I decided that I wasn't going to do anything! Screw working! I mean it was only going to get me thirteen days off my ninety day sentence so I decided to boycott and let them send me back to the general population to do my entire time in my one man cell, where I didn't have to be bothered with anyone but myself.

Well, things, as always, didn't go the way I wanted them to go. They wouldn't send me back! At all! So, there I sat, on my bunk, mad, for days on end, trying to do as little as possible. During that time of sitting and thinking, I had the opportunity to talk with some of the other men that were in similar situations like myself. What we decided was that there was only one way to break and change this cycle that, like so many others, we were in and sure to continue to repeat, we would need to come up with a "sure fire" plan, and we needed to work the plan. The problem was, NO ONE KNEW WHAT THE PLAN SHOULD BE!

After sitting and contemplating what needed to be done to break this cycle, not just for me, but also for my children and grandchildren, I realized a few things. One thing was that due to my criminal history and convictions a.k.a. "strikes", I needed "letters" a.k.a. degree(s) behind my name versus "strikes". So educating myself in an area that could bring me high wages and or allow me to start my own business was the first thing on my list. So I had to get into college in a field that was "FELONY FRIENDLY" and also would be something that I didn't already know how to do, so HVAC was the choice. So I did all that I could to get into college.

The second thing was to learn a skilled trade that would do one of two things—1, earn me a HIGH wage ADULT income, or 2, allow me the opportunity to create and run my own business.

The third part of the plan was to use that education, use those skills learned, and network both into long-term earning potential and experience. I had estimated that these three steps would take or need to be accomplished over a seven to ten year time span. The second half of the twenty year plan was set up to gather and amass as many resources and funds as possible. I figured that once I had come to the end of this 20 year plan that I would be able to live a very nice life, provide for my mate, and set my children and grandchildren's futures on a successful path.

The tricky part of this plan is the part where you learn how much discipline and patience you have or DON'T have. See I learned through reading about the successful "process of elimination" and "cause and effect" that you must be very patient and very diligent to be successful. And with enough time, knowledge, and funding, there's nothing you can't accomplish.

So you must figure out what it is you want/love to do! You must learn all that you can about HOW to do it! And then, at some point, you must have the COURAGE to ACTUALLY do it! Then you should learn how to market it in a way that others would like to repeat your process while paying you for the knowledge you have taught and or given them. Once you get to this point, there is no limit to what you can do, not only in your lifetime, but also, for your future generations of loved ones, be it family, friends, or community.

So how does one learn to be patient? For me, it took a lot of looking at and being honest with myself! I had to be honest about what I ate, what I did, what I wasn't doing, who was helping me do it or not helping me do things that would be in-line with what I was trying to accomplish all while adding positivity into the universe. I had to look at what I was buying, not buying, reading, and saying.

The truth in this assessment of self was not an easy pill to swallow! When you're out here depressed because you don't have money, the first thing you do is spend money on things you can't afford, i.e. partying, drinking, smoking, sex etc. What I learned is that slowly, but surely, when you change to be a better person, your circle of people changes. As I quit doing the things that were not making life better, the less often people wanted to be around me. I wasn't the "FUN", "PARTY" person anymore. I didn't want to be in a room full of drunken, high, and depressed people.

As soon as I did though I also noticed the positivity of what I was doing. I started meeting people that were actually ACTIVELY pursuing their dreams! They weren't drunk all day every day. They weren't high. They were usually happy and looking forward to getting up and doing something towards their dreams!

This inspired me! It fueled my desire to want to create my

own business and have control over my own life. I wanted more! It seemed as though the more I did to make my life better, the more I came in contact with those who wanted to make my dreams and goals come to fruition.

This didn't come without its own problems. You lose those people that you've known for quite a while. You lose those people that you have become comfortable with being and having around you. You even lose those people who you thought loved you and would always have your back. Happiness and success come at a cost! Few will ever be able to afford nor will even want to pay the price. It was, and still is, from time to time, difficult to "WAIT" for life, success, and peace of mind, to catch up with your desires. It is, however, worth it!

In order to stay on task, a few things to do are: find others that are doing what you love to do, and, get mentored, or ask for leads on someone who will be willing to help you. Also, utilize your daily planner. Probably the most important thing you can do is to TAKE A BREAK! You have to give your mind, body, and spirit to recharge, so plan time to be away from chasing down your dream(s). No seed ever became a tree overnight!

Are You Your Biggest Cheerleader Or Your Own Biggest Hater (Be Positive)

ONE HARD THING about being patient enough is remaining positive. It is hard to watch other people being successful all while you are still going through your struggle. Not doing this (remaining positive) causes jealousy, envy, hatred, depression, and anger. You can become successful while being angry, but, you won't be happy and your business will carry that energy with it, and you don't want that.

Plan out time for positive thoughts and affirmations. I started out with doing positive things since it takes and uses less energy to be positive than it does to be negative. It has been noted by professionals that it takes about eleven positive thoughts to counteract one, JUST ONE SINGLE NEGATIVE THOUGHT! The thing about thinking positively is you start to act, behave, and ATTRACT other positive vibes, people, and things into your life. Doing so creates a circle or ripple of positivity around you and all you come in contact with. This ripple will continue to grow larger and hopefully wash over that inevitable moment that you will encounter that negative person, place, or thing! But for a moment, let's be clear, sometimes we actually need those moments too. There will be times when the negative will challenge you. It'll make you question your purpose, focus, direction, and even your very existence! And trust me, It'll be really bad when you have a moment, those moments that'll have you so shook that you'll want to consider ending your own life! I know this because I've been right there on the edge of the abyss, ready to dive in, head first, with a sweet ass swan dive, being the means to my own end. Fortunately, at that moment, that look into the darkness, put me into a position to make a decision on which way to live my life. I was at a "CROSSROAD" moment. I was at that moment where you quit, and disappoint everyone that loves you, or, you choose to live and honor them, by living a life worth sharing your story with others. So, I decided to jump into that darkness! What?! You thought this was going to be one of those "FEEL GOOD" STORIES?! I did try to end my life. Fortunately though, The Holy Universe decided my life had better meaning and purpose. From that moment on I knew there had to be a higher purpose for me living or that I just really was too dumb to know how to end my own life. Looking back, I realized that the answer was—a little bit of both.

So what did I do? I changed my circle! I stopped hanging around with people that weren't doing positive things. Doing so showed me that I was not only strong enough to LIVE, but strong enough to live WELL, and to be a blessing to others. I was having success in all the little moments that

I encountered. People started noticing, and when I was asked, I did the same thing I did when I was telling myself negative things—I spoke on it! The more I did, the better my life became and just like I did, YOU CAN TOO!

Surround yourself with band members and you'll not only be able to blow your own horn, but, you'll also have a great circle of people to make beautiful music with!

Do As I Say. . . .
(Be And Stay Positive)

ONE OF THE easiest ways to stay positive is by helping others stay positive. Volunteering your time and resources shows others that you're not just talking, but, actually walking the walk. For some strange reason, folks tend to LIKE when you're already doing what you're talking about. It lends more weight to the message you're sharing or trying to share.

I've always tried to live by the thought process of, "If the situation was reversed. . . .", this gave me a different perspective on things. It taught me that I could be ok thinking outside the box. This also kept me honest in my position when giving out assessments because the first time you give someone some advice, they're going to ask you, "so what would you do?" or " why didn't YOU do this?". It is always better and easier to be honest in answering, "I am!" or "I did!" versus standing there looking dazed, confused, and speechless.

In the hood, people without guidance look for those who are strong and smart, and they are looking to be led. They want to do what they see being done, so if they see bad or good, that's what they will imitate.

Showing others that you are doing what you are telling them about helps to instill hope that things can and WILL be better. So always walk the walk that you talk! This concept isn't just about character traits. This also applies to money and being healthy both mentally and physically. Like in a previous chapter, if you're saying to people that one of the roads to success is showing discipline in one's actions then this should go for how you save and or spend your hard earned cash.

You can't be out here blowing your money on rims, clothes, and gym shoes, then needing someone to loan you $20 for gas money. People should be seeing you growing by means of smart money investments. Even before that, until you get to where you want to be, people should be setting budgets in an effort to secure their futures financially.

One of the hardest things for most people to do in their lives is to delay gratification! One of the main trappings of those that are at or below poverty level is the process of as soon as you get a large lump sum of cash, i.e. tax refund, student loan check, work bonus etc., they go out and spend it on things that don't accumulate value. This supplies them with a temporary high or euphoria, but, once that wears off, folks are right back to working out of that hole to get to the next high.

There once was a simple study done that involved children and marshmallows. It was a simple premise; a room full of kids, a bag of marshmallows, and time. The idea and offer was this: you can get your marshmallows now or get more if you wait. Let's just say a lot of the kids went home early and there was an excess of marshmallows left. It's the same way with adults! Most can't wait to eat those marshmallows! They want them right now! They can't see the huge pay off of the stash of marshmallows just beyond your view.

In order to be successful, you need to be patient and be seen being patient. This grows your gratitude and eliminates anyone being able to have negative words or attitudes with you.

Always Be Polite! Even To The Assholes (Stay Humble)

HAVE YOU EVER heard someone say, "he is doing great, but, he's an asshole! Let's give him some money!" You probably haven't. I know I haven't heard that said. If I do ever hear that though I'll be writing another book on "How To Be An A'Hole So People Will Give You Money!" Until then, people love people who are out here helping others and doing it out of the kindness of their own heart.

No one HAS to be nice, but, of all the things in this world to be, why be a jerk? One of the easiest ways to be a blessing is by understanding the plight of others and knowing that things could be worse and probably are for someone else. Remember the story of the man who had no shoes meeting the man who had no feet? Well he had just come from WALKING with a man who had no legs and WALKED around on his hands! Everything is perspective!

One way to always keep yourself in check is to always ask yourself, "did I say please?" and, "did I say thank you?"

Doing this, and being sincere in doing this, helps to keep you humble and shows appreciation to the person and or people you are interacting with.

Whenever I needed something and had to ask my wife to take care of it, it always was followed up with "please" and "thank you". I did this so that she knew that no matter what it was that I needed her to do of whatever I needed from her, whether it be big or small, I appreciated that she did it. In this world of selfish people, someone doing something for you, out of the kindness of their heart, often times even when they don't want to even be bothered, is a big thing no matter how small of a thing that it actually is. The act that is being extended to you should be acknowledged.

As a leader, someone that wants to be a success in their field, acknowledgement goes a long way. We all can be bosses bossing others around, but, successful leaders are those that coach, inspire, and acknowledge their stars, as well as, those that struggle but show they are working hard to be better.

Saying 'please" and "thank you" shows that you want to involve them in the decision making process and you are happy that they chose to assist you with whatever you have asked of them.

When it comes to dealing with the "assholes" of the world, there is an old saying of, "kill'em with kindness!" This philosophy works often in multiple ways. One thing it does is, it takes away their power as a bully. Most people are rude jerks because they have negative issues going on in their day and or life that hasn't been dealt with which causes a negative projection of energy towards others. Saying "please" and "thank you" deflates those negative energies and sends positive energy back to them. Hopefully, with enough kindness returned to the sender, hopefully, their behavior will improve.

Another thing that happens over time and with repeated kindness, is you turn a hater into an ally versus an enemy. Now this isn't always the case since there are some folks who will never try to resolve their issues so they'll carry their negative baggage for life.

Remember, though life and success is based on how you react to adversity, not how "assholes" act towards you. One of the last things that saying "please" and "thank you" to "assholes" does is, it re-enforces your level of discipline, patience, and love, because GOD knows it takes all of those things to keep you from slapping the hell out of someone with a bad attitude!

So remember, whether it is during a good or a bad situation, always stay humble and always say "please" and "thank you"! It may just create a new friend, business partner, relationship, or just keep you from being arrested for assault and battery! Be someone's ray of sunshine, their hope, and just know that you are blessed and have the ability to change the world, regardless of the obstacles or assholes.

Can You Even Find A Hat For That Head (Ego)

O K YOU'VE GOT some movement going on. You're out here helping people. Someone, hell, quite a few people have thanked you and have expressed to you how you have made a difference in their life. It feels good doesn't it? Well guess what, it's supposed to feel good! You've put positive energy out here into the Universe! Now what? The buzz from that high has worn off, there's no more people to help at the moment, and no funding coming in to move forward. What comes next is the same thing that comes after getting high—THE CRASH.

You've felt the good feelings and you want to feel it again! You're searching for more people to help. Voila! You've found the contact that has given you your larger buzz and this time it's a long buzz. More people are coming to you seeking your knowledge, your help, and thanking you. You're loving this feeling like you are the expert that knows it all in the area that you are speaking about. Here's the problem, you think you know it all and you can't help but to make sure others know that you know it all!

Success, it amplifies the personal characteristics of the individual, and most people are very egotistical beings, simply because most have been programmed to believe that you are not "liked" if you are not successful. So when we do become successful and start to gain a bit of notoriety, it goes right to most people's head. Remember though, part of becoming and staying successful is being and staying humble. Remembering that you didn't gain success on your own, but with the help of many others, both directly and indirectly.

One must remember the purpose of even being successful is to not only help ourselves, but to help others, and to do it without being concerned with whether they can return the help. Remember, that to become and to stay a success, one must understand that there will be cycles of change, both pleasant and horribly bad type of changes. If you allow yourself to become addicted to the highs and not comfortable with the lessons of the lows, then buddy, you're going to start to hear the "hissing". If you ignore the "hissing" and keep boosting yourself up to be more than who you are or more than what you can actually do, then you are going to find yourself in a really bad place when someone pulls out that sharp, pointy pin and with the slightest of a touch to your inflated ego, you're going to hear the biggest pop ever! And it won't just be you that will hear it, it'll be all those people that you've sold a false reality to, that'll be there to bear witness to the bursting of your giant air head, and it'll all be because you forgot rule number seven—STAY HUMBLE!

Our responsibility is to be leaders of hope, success, and LOVE. We can only do that by being bullies through hate, or by being leaders through LOVE. The moment you choose hate, just know that the UNIVERSE loves to pop big headed air balloons, so keep your ego in check and always remember to stay humble.

Your Net-Work Is Your Net-Worth! (Network)

So how does one get started out here on their road to success? Well, if you have made the decision to go down this road versus choosing to go the other route of doing things on your own, then the first or next step is to start looking for people who may be interested in hearing your story or helping you out with whatever it is that you're trying to do or get done.

This may be a really short chapter because the simplest way to explain this philosophy is to simply say, LOOK FOR THE PERSON, PEOPLE, OR ENTITY that is successfully doing what you want to do, and somehow, get them to help you, or see if they would be willing to share some information with you.

Attend all the events that bring you into the space of the people and information that you need. Talk to everyone that may be able to connect you to that information. When you run out of events to attend, groups to join on social media sites like Facebook, Instagram, Twitter, and LinkedIn, then you need to just step outside your comfort zone and just start reaching out to people—DIRECTLY!

The worst thing that can happen is that you are told no or not answered. The best thing that can happen is, someone could be willing to help you accomplish your dreams! So remember, it only takes one yes to change your life and that could happen at any time, and in an instant.

So while you are out here networking, learn the names, the business, the nuances, the reasons why others have failed doing what you want to do, what you can offer, and carry yourself like you have already been told yes, and you will have the life and things you want, and you will be able to help those you love, as well as, others who need your help, hope, strength, knowledge, leadership, and LOVE.

Excuse Me Brutha But Errrruh, You Got Some Spare Change (Giving)

HAVE YOU EVER gone to the gas station or the corner store and even before you can reach the door, there are dudes begging for YOUR "spare change"? I mean like really, what is "spare change", and why would I just give it away, to some random person, standing around, wasting their precious time, begging others, for what they have worked hard to have?

There are times in this life when you'll be approached for help from those people that see your "giving" heart as a weakness. They think that you are a softy, or even worse a sucker for a good sob story. Nowadays these people don't even have a good sob story. They are just coming straight out the box with, "hey man, I'm just tryna get enough change for a beer and a few loosies!" Beware of all of these con artist! Shoot them down quick! Not literally though, that wouldn't be cool no matter how much they may deserve it for this foolishness!

On the other hand though, throughout this life, especially when you're making decisions and taking actions to make your life better, you will cross paths with others whose situations are simply tragic, and even worse, just plain FUCKED UP! You'll know for sure that they need help by the simple fact that they're situation is really bad, and they are trying to fix it but they won't ask anyone to suffer with them or ask anyone for help. These people, are the ones who need your "spare change".

When you give of yourself to someone that truly needs help, and you do it without expectation of anything in return, you positively affect the Universe. Giving to others causes physical changes to your body, literally, giving you life.

Giving to others, creates a humbleness within us that helps us appreciate what we have and what we have gone through and survived. It makes you appreciate having both legs when you are playing basketball with a guy that is scoring more points than you, even though he has a prosthetic leg. It makes you appreciate the colors of flowers when you see the vivid paintings of a rainbow by a woman that has been blind since being a child. It makes you appreciate sitting down to a dinner table when you see others serving the homeless.

You can never be TOO hopeful to those in need. As you help others, you unleash energies in the Universe that respond to selfless acts. And though we don't give as a means of negotiation with God-the Holy Universe, we are rewarded for those actions of not being selfish.

So when you have a chance to help others who can do nothing for you in return, GIVE! Give beyond your capacity. You will be changing a life and the Universe itself. The reality is this: if you follow these steps, you will have far more than you could have imagined before reading this book! The thing is, you can't take it with you. However, you can keep recycling it and using it to continue to help yourself and your family and even beyond your own household, you can help others. Doing this will make everything around you better and more positive. This will cause your light to shine on others, outshining the darkness of your own mistakes.

Just understand that you will have moments—crossroads—where decisions you have made, caused mistakes and now, decisions have to be made that will no longer allow you to go backwards. These decisions, at this crossroad, will either have you on the path to further turmoil, or, on the pathway to peace, LOVE, and success. The choice is yours. You've F'd Up! Now What?!

End

www.ingramcontent.com/pod-product-compliance
Lightning Source LLC
Chambersburg PA
CBHW051412290426
44108CB00015B/2261